YOUR GUIDE TO

Spe Salvi: Saved in Hope

BENEDICT XVI MADE SIMPLE

YOUR GUIDE TO
Spe Salvi: Saved in Hope

by Barry Michaels

auline
BOOKS & MEDIA
Boston

Library of Congress Cataloging-in-Publication Data

Michaels, Barry.
  Your guide to Spe salvi : saved in hope / by Barry Michaels.
    p. cm. — (Benedict the XVI made simple)
  ISBN 0-8198-8808-7 (pbk.)
  1. Catholic Church. Pope (2005- : Benedict XVI). Spe salvi. 2. Hope—Religious
aspects—Catholic Church. 3. Catholic Church—Doctrines. I. Title.
BX1795.H69C3836 2008
234'.25—dc22

                                                        2008025282

Papal text copyright © Libreria Editrice Vaticana, Città del Vaticano

Papal coat of arms: www.agnusimages.com

Excerpts from *Eschatology: Death and Eternal Life*, used with permission: the
Catholic University of Amercia Press, Wahington, D.C.

Cover design by Rosana Usselmann

Published by Pauline Books & Media, 50 Saint Paul's Avenue, Boston, MA
02130-3491 www.pauline.org.

Printed in the U.S.A.

Pauline Books & Media is the publishing house of the Daughters of St. Paul, an
international congregation of women religious serving the Church with the com-
munications media.

1 2 3 4 5 6 7 8 9   13 12 11 10 09 08

This is dedicated to Abigail Anne,
born into our family and baptized
into the family of God
during the time I was writing this little book.
She is a living and wonderful image of hope,
for whom I, my wife, and
Abigail's older brothers and sisters
give thanks to God.

Contents

Preface.. *1*

Acknowledgment... *5*

A Prayer Before Reading *Spe Salvi*......................... *6*

Section One
Introduction *7*

Section Two
Faith Is Hope... *12*

Section Three
The Concept of Faith-Based Hope
in the New Testament and the Early Church.............. *22*

Section Four
Eternal Life: What Is It? *31*

Section Five
Is Christian Hope Individualistic? *38*

Section Six

The Transformation of Christian Faith:
Hope in the Modern Age *44*

Section Seven

The True Shape of Christian Hope *55*

Section Eight

Settings for Learning and Practicing Hope................ *63*

    I. Prayer as a School of Hope............................ *63*

    II. Action and Suffering
        as Settings for Learning Hope........................ *67*

    III. Judgment as a Setting
         for Learning and Practicing Hope *74*

Section Nine

Mary, Star of Hope....................................... *80*

Notes *84*

Preface

I suppose it's unavoidable. When someone mentions hope, I do *not* think first of the virtue. I think of my daughter, whose name is Hope. I'll tell you why.

When she was born, my wife and I had suffered a series of personal and professional failures and frustrations. Life had battered us with some severe blows. Even our attempts to move beyond the frustrations into new, more promising directions were met with failure. So when our daughter was born in the midst of this dour time, we didn't have to think very hard about what to name her. We could use a little hope around the house, we told each other.

Hope is six years old now—and wonderful. And while we still face struggles, as everyone does, many things have greatly improved since her birth. We have moved into a different season of our lives and are thankful for it.

What makes the difference?

But what if things had not improved? What if the downward trend had continued? What if the circumstances of our lives had grown still more painful, frustrating, and sad?

Despite our difficulties, it's easy to think of worse things that could have befallen us. Suppose, God forbid, they had.

I'd like to think my marriage would survive even the most desperate situation. I believe it would. But then, I've never been that far down such a dark road, and other people, good people, have thrown away a lot more—even life itself—along that road.

What makes the difference in such circumstances? What is it that carries some folks through the darkness, even the longest and most dismal darkness, to the other side, all the while being able to discern meaning to life, meaning despite the pain, even meaning *in* the pain? What gives some people the unshakable conviction that there is always something more, something better, something worth waiting and struggling for? Even more, what gives them the awareness of something and Someone who always awaits them—and which ultimately provides a sublime joy in the midst of it all? Pope Benedict XVI provides answers to these and similar questions in his encyclical letter *Spe Salvi*, on the virtue of Christian hope.

In presenting hope as the answer to these questions, the Pope is not using the word as it is most commonly used, as when a teen looks out her bedroom window on a snowy night and says, "I hope school is canceled tomorrow." That is natural hope. That kind of hope cannot offer what the Pope describes in the brief introductory paragraph of his encyclical: "we have been given hope, trustworthy hope, by virtue of which we can face our present: the present, even if it is arduous, can be lived and accepted if it leads towards a goal, if we can be sure of this goal, and if this goal is great enough to justify the effort of the journey" (no. 1).

This is a supernatural hope. It's the hope of the Psalmist who prayed, "The Lord is my shepherd, I shall not want.... Even though I walk through the darkest valley, I fear no evil; for you are with me" (Ps 23:1, 4).

Benedict by the Numbers

Now some numbers.

Seven. That's the number of philosophers from outside the Catholic tradition whose thinking Pope Benedict weaves into the text of *Spe Salvi*, the second encyclical of his pontificate. Few other encyclicals in Church history, if any, explicitly refer to the work of so many non-Catholic thinkers. The Pope is not afraid to draw upon and even point out what is good outside his own tradition.

Zero. That's the number of times Pope Benedict's encyclical cites the documents of the Second Vatican Council or the voluminous writings of his predecessor, Pope John Paul II. Every other encyclical published since the Second Vatican Council ended has cited its teaching, usually many times. To take this as some kind of "conservative" rejection of the Council or of John Paul II, as some have tried to do, is disingenuous. Others have suggested it's an expression of Benedict's conviction that Vatican II is just one aspect of a long and rich history of Church teaching. At the very least it suggests that the Pope has confidence in his own teaching of fundamental Christian doctrine and does not feel bound to present it in the way some may expect.

Four. That's the number of languages, other than English, that readers will encounter as they work through *Spe Salvi*.

Although with this letter the Pope addresses not only bishops and theologians, but also all the lay faithful, there is not a hint of talking down to anyone. Instead, he seems to assume that readers will be willing to carefully think their way through some challenging explanations and illustrations.

That is what we propose to do. And as we do so, we'll have the company of saints such as Paul, Mary, Bernard of Clairvaux, Thomas Aquinas, and Francis of Assisi, who have been revered for centuries. But Benedict also introduces us to some more recent saints who are new to the Church's life and liturgy. Josephine Bakhita and Paul Le-Bao-Tinh were both canonized by John Paul II and deserve to be much more widely known.

Did I mention Augustine? He is here, too, most emphatically. St. Augustine of Hippo, the great Doctor of the Church from fourth-century North Africa, whom the Pope has taken as a spiritual-intellectual godfather since he was a young priest, shows up nine times in this encyclical. Though Benedict is presenting the ancient faith as it has been passed on through the centuries, he has not hesitated to make this letter a very personal expression of the truths it contains.

To sum up, reading *Spe Salvi* will fascinate, challenge, and reward anyone willing to make the effort to read and think through it. This companion will allow readers to get more out of the letter—not dumbing it down in any way, but fleshing out its topics, providing a bit more background information, and offering a few helpful illustrations. Benedict will be our teacher, and he offers us the kind of teaching that, when it really sinks in, can change a life.

You can count on it.

Acknowledgment

Public thanks are overdue to Sr. Marianne Lorraine Trouvé, FSP, a gifted editor whose many insightful suggestions have made my work much better than it would otherwise be on this project and in each of my previous books.

A Prayer Before Reading
Spe Salvi

Come, Holy Spirit.
Make my time with this encyclical holy time.
May it not be simply interesting or inspiring reading,
but may it draw me deeper into the mystery of God
and his action in the world.
Help me to understand what I read.
Teach me what you want me to learn.
Help it to sink into my heart as well as my mind,
that my faith as well as my knowledge may grow.
And give me the wisdom and the courage
   to live it out.
Come, Holy Spirit.
Amen.

Introduction

Spe Salvi, published on November 30, 2007, is Pope Benedict's second encyclical. His first, *Deus Caritas Est* (published almost a year earlier), is on the topic of Christian love. It seems safe to say that the Pope intends to provide us with a trilogy of encyclicals on the three theological virtues: faith, hope, and love. Some explanation may help.

Virtues 101

Virtues guide our moral lives. They help us to choose what is good. Moral choices keep us from being like a rudderless boat turning this way and that, bobbing aimlessly on the waves. Although there is no "official" list of all the virtues, most of us could list dozens: patience, honesty, purity, kindness, compassion, courage, tolerance, generosity, and so on.

Each of those just mentioned, and most of the others we might name, are known as *human virtues*. The four primary human virtues are prudence, justice, temperance, and fortitude.

They're called the cardinal virtues, from the Latin *cardo* or hinge, because the practice of all other virtues hinges upon these four. Human virtues are the "moral muscles" we use to do the work of moral choosing and acting. Like physical muscles, they grow stronger when we use them (or weaker when we don't). The more I act patiently, the more patient a person I become. The less frequently I am generous, the weaker I grow in the virtue of generosity.

Keeping with the muscles analogy, we can note that sometimes the circumstances of life call for "heavy lifting," serious and difficult moral choices. If I face such a circumstance with moral muscles that have grown weak through lack of use, it's unlikely they'll be up to the greater challenge when needed.

These human virtues are not exclusive to Catholicism or any other religion, or, for that matter, to religion at all. Aristotle wrote about the virtues three centuries before the birth of Jesus. Without the human virtues, no one, of any religion, could act morally.

But in Christian tradition, there is another category of virtues, known as the *theological virtues*. These three virtues—faith, hope, and love—are unique.

Unlike the human virtues, the theological virtues are *received rather than achieved*. While we grow in the human virtues by acting virtuously (exercising those "muscles"), these three virtues come to us only as a gift from God, poured out by the Holy Spirit. (Thus they are also known as the *infused* virtues.) At the same time, it would be a mistake to say we have no part to play in whether we are people of faith or hope or love. A gift isn't a gift until the person receiving the gift accepts it. The theological virtues work in us only to the extent that we open ourselves to the gift.

In fact, the Pope makes clear in his introduction that hope (and we could say the same of faith and love) is inseparable from redemption, the salvation God offers us in Christ. That, too, is pure gift. And we must willingly receive and respond to that gift for it to be effective in us.

So St. Paul could write the words with which the Pope opens his letter and which give it its name: "*'Spe Salvi facti sumus'*—in hope we were saved" (Rom 8:24). Clearly, hope is crucial. More than a question of what gets us through the rough spots of life, important as that is, we're talking about a matter of our eternal salvation. *what is meant by this?*

Reflection Questions

1. At what moments in your life have you most needed the virtue of hope? At those times, what difference did hope make?

2. Have you known personally any people who seemed to have lost all hope? Have *you* ever experienced real despair, an utter absence of hope? How did this manifest itself, what did it look like, in your daily life?

3. As you begin reading this encyclical, what will be the biggest challenge for you? Have you ever read a papal document such as this before? Is there any chance you will approach it with a negative attitude about Church teaching in general or toward this Pope in particular? Or will it simply be difficult to set aside the time to read it and to give it some serious

thought? How can you prepare your heart to receive what God is saying to you through Benedict's words?

Prayer Prompts

1. *A prayer of thanksgiving:* As we noted above, hope is a theological virtue. It's a gift we receive, not a habit or attitude we achieve. Supernatural hope is a grace, freely given by God, and it ordinarily comes first of all in our Baptism. Pray a prayer of thanksgiving to God for the gift received.

2. *A prayer of supplication:* Pray for a deepening of the gift of hope, for the Spirit both to pour out the gift upon you more abundantly and to make your heart more open to receive the gift and more docile to its power, that hope may become more active in your life.

3. *A prayer of intercession:* Pray for those who are without hope, certainly for anyone you know personally, but also for the walking wounded throughout the world who are experiencing profound despair. Pray that through the Spirit's action in them, they will open themselves to and receive the gift of hope. (And remind yourself, as you offer this prayer, that the phrase, "there but for the grace of God go I," is quite literally true in this case.)

Putting It into Practice

The Pope emphasizes from the beginning to the end of this encyclical that the virtue of hope has real consequences and makes a real difference in the lives of individual Christians. In the pages ahead, we will consider many ways that this can happen.

For now, simply commit yourself to reading through this letter that the Pope has written to the whole Church, and give some thought to the time you'll set aside for doing this. Consider scheduling your daily "appointment" with the Pope, in the same way you might reserve time for important business or social activities. You might want to make it part of your regular prayer time, or share this time with others—a spouse or group of fellow Christians.

Be aware as you begin: Benedict does not write in quick and easy "sound bites." He guides us carefully through explanations and arguments, trusting us enough to make the effort to follow him. That takes a certain amount of attentiveness and reflection. One hallmark of his ministry as pope is that Benedict is a master teacher. He has often conducted informal question-and-answer sessions, for example, with a wide variety of audiences—priests, teenagers, young children—since his election. But we must be willing to be cooperative and attentive students.

Be assured, the effort will bear great fruit.

Faith Is Hope

When I teach the virtues in my high school religion classes, I introduce hope by asking what the word means. Invariably, as I field responses from a handful of students, the word *faith* quickly begins creeping into their definitions. "It's faith that something is going to happen." "It's having faith that you'll get something you want."

It seems odd, at first, to use one virtue to define another. But my students are not being lazy with their definitions. In fact, Pope Benedict does the same thing.

Faith and Hope

Opening this first major section of his letter, the Pope begins to explore hope as it's presented in the pages of the Bible. He reaches the interesting conclusion that, in many places, "the words faith and hope seem interchangeable." We see it in two ways. First, the significant ways in which hope and faith are explicitly presented together; second, the way hope is written about as if it were the same as faith.

At times they are presented together — not like two people in the same room are together, but like two lungs in one chest are together, doing the same job and existing as the same organ. Here the Pope points to the close connection between the two virtues in Hebrews 10:22–23, which calls upon Christians to approach God "in full assurance of faith" and to "hold fast to the confession of our hope without wavering, for he who has promised is faithful." We also shouldn't miss the sentence that comes up just a few verses later in the same letter: "Now faith is the assurance of things hoped for, the conviction of things not seen" (Heb 11:1). Like my students (but in reverse) the author of Hebrews is defining *faith* by referring to *hope*.

We also see this close interconnection between faith and hope in St. Paul's frequent insistence that people who are without faith (in Jesus and especially in his resurrection) are therefore without hope. The Pope cites here First Thessalonians 4:13 ("But we do not want you to be uninformed, brothers and sisters, about those who have died, so that you may not grieve as others do who have no hope"), and Ephesians 2:12 ("remember that you were at that time without Christ … having no hope and without God in the world"). It's in First Corinthians 15:17–19, too, where Paul speaks about the hope flowing from Christ's resurrection.

We could multiply examples of New Testament passages where faith and hope are explicitly connected, doing the same job. There's Second Corinthians 5:5–7, where Paul insists that "we are always confident [or, we always have hope] … for we walk by faith, not by sight." And in a beautiful way, Paul sees the great faith of Abraham (who is, after all, the Old Testament's quintessential "man of faith") as *one with his hope:* "Hoping against hope, he believed that he would become 'the father of many nations,' according to what was said, 'So numerous shall your descendants be'" (Rom 4:18).

In addition to these many explicit connections of faith and hope in the Bible, the New Testament also presents hope as *functioning* in the same way that faith does. The passage from which *Spe Salvi* takes its title is one example. Here it is, with the verses that surround it:

> We know that the whole creation has been groaning in labor pains until now; and not only creation, but we ourselves, who have the first fruits of the Spirit, groan inwardly while we wait for adoption, the redemption of our bodies. For in hope we were saved. Now hope that is seen is not hope. For who hopes for what is seen? But if we hope for what we do not see, we wait for it with patience. (Rom 8: 22–25)

And the Pope also points us to First Peter 3:15: "Always be ready to make your defense to anyone who demands from you an accounting for the hope that is in you."

Besides these examples, recall Paul's dramatic claim, found in two different places in Acts (23:6 and 26:6), that he and the early Church were being persecuted *for their hope* (as opposed to their faith?) in the resurrection.

In the Bible, says the Pope, "Hope is equivalent to faith." It's put even plainer in this section's heading: "Faith Is Hope." Later, he'll also use the term "Christian faith-hope." And so, with St. Paul, we can say the very same thing about hope that the Bible says about faith: by it, we are saved.

"Come, Lord Jesus!"

We shouldn't be surprised, then, that this kind of faith marked the life of the community that produced the New Testament in the first place. "The self-understanding of the early Christians was shaped by their having received the gift of trustworthy hope," the Pope writes.

One of the earliest recorded Christian prayers is (in Greek) *Marana tha!* "Come, Lord Jesus!" Paul prays it in First Corinthians 16:22, and John prays it in Revelation 22:20. The prayer suggests that the first Christians looked forward to the coming of Christ and prayed for it with a sort of longing. In other words, their hope was strong.

How do we think about the Second Coming of Christ? If we do at all, it's likely with discomfort and even fear. Though we hear at every Mass that we're "waiting in joyful hope" for it to happen, have these words of the prayer—"Come, Lord Jesus!" —worked their way very deeply into our hearts?

What did the first Christians know that we may have forgotten? We will explore that question—and the consequences of forgetting—with the Pope in the following pages.

From Nothing to Nothing

In nihil ab nihilo quam cito recidimus. "How quickly we fall back from nothing to nothing." Benedict cites this "pagan" epitaph dating from the birth of Christianity to illustrate a point Paul makes about the situation of those who worshipped other gods. But in many ways it applies just as well to us today. That Latin word *nihil* ("nothing") gives us the term for a common way of looking at reality today: *nihilism*. (Literally, that's "nothing-ism.")

Nihilism sprang up in the world of philosophy more than a century ago. It's most often associated with Friedrich Nietzsche. But it's more than an idea on the pages of books. We sometimes see it more clearly—and disastrously—in the lives of people around us.

When people treat their lives and choices as if they had no meaning, when they act as if human beings were no different from animals, when they suggest that there is nothing we "should" or "should not" do, but we can freely do whatever we feel like—that is nihilism. Nihilism is seeing life as an empty sequence of events without purpose, without cause, without direction, and, unavoidably then, without hope.

Christianity offers something dramatically different. The Pope writes that "a distinguishing mark of Christians" is "the fact that they have a future: it is not that they know the details of what awaits them, but they know in general terms that their life will not end in emptiness" (no. 2).

And that makes an enormous difference in our experience of life itself. That truth, the Pope says, "makes things happen and is life-changing. The dark door of time, of the future, has been thrown open. The one who has hope lives differently; the one who hopes has been granted the gift of a new life" (no. 2).

No wonder from the beginning people called it "Good News."

A Living Example

It's one thing to discuss Greek terminology or modern philosophy; it is entirely another to see hope incarnated in the flesh-and-blood experience of a woman for whom the difference meant everything. Pope Benedict concludes this section by offering us a real-life example of Christian hope.

St. Josephine Bakhita is one of the Church's newest saints. Pope John Paul II canonized her during the Jubilee Year 2000. As with all saints, if we think of St. Bakhita more as a plaster statue standing silently with eyes raised to heaven than as a living, breathing person like ourselves, we do her an injustice and deprive ourselves of the drama of her witness.

It may be helpful to supplement the brief biography the Pope offers in his letter. Born in Darfur in the Sudan, Bakhita was kidnapped as a child and sold and resold into brutal slavery before reaching adulthood. She ended up being bought and taken to Italy by an Italian government official, who then passed her on to another family, the Michielis. In fact, it was in taking the Michielis' young daughter, Mimminato, to school each day that Bakhita heard the message that offered her the hope she had never dreamed was possible.

Each day Bakhita would bring Mimminato to the school run by the Daughters of Charity. As she waited in the back of the classroom, she overheard the religion lessons and ultimately came to embrace faith in Christ. Eventually she was baptized. Later, after winning her freedom through the court system in Venice, she became a Daughter of Charity herself.

Bakhita's words quoted by Benedict are a vibrant example of what hope is all about: "I am definitively loved and whatever happens to me—I am awaited by this Love. And so my life is good" (no. 3). That verb, *awaited*, carries a profound meaning. (Benedict uses it three times in one paragraph.) Josephine knew that we can look forward to something better following the difficulties of life. But more: she knew that *Someone* is with us in the midst of life and awaits us at the end of it. In comments Pope John Paul II made to the pilgrims gathered in Rome for Bakhita's beatification in 1992, he spoke of her hope, saying,

> Blessed Josephine Bakhita, in her humility and her total abandonment to God, teaches us not only to work and to pray, but above all to trust. Through her tragic experiences, she learned, by God's grace, to have complete faith in him, that he is present always and everywhere, and to be therefore good and generous, constantly and toward everyone.... She saw, that is, the providential hand of the Most High, who guides and sustains human history, never abandoning those who trust in him, even if many times he allows us to pass through dark and impenetrable circumstances.[1]

A Suffering People

But Pope Benedict could have chosen from hundreds of great saints to illustrate the difference that Christian hope can make in a person's life. His choice of Bakhita was surely not a random one.

In our own day, the people of Darfur, Bakhita's homeland, have suffered through years of terrible injustice. The government of the Sudan (of which Darfur is one region) has led a genocide against this people within its own borders. The international community has done very little to intervene, and the atrocities committed were ignored for many years by the world media, which have only recently begun to acknowledge a problem. In this situation, despair would be a painfully easy option.

In 1992, Pope John Paul II took the occasion of Bakhita's beatification to draw the attention of the Church and the world to the plight of the people of Darfur. He also tried to make it a moment in which the people there might know that the Church stood with them and, in some way, suffered with them.

Less than a year later, John Paul II traveled personally to the Sudan. At a special Mass in honor of Josephine Bakhita, held in the capital city Khartoum, the Pope said:

> Her Beatification was an act of respect not only for her but also for the Sudan, since *a daughter of this land was put forward as a hero of mercy and of goodwill.* ... The immense suffering of millions of innocent victims impels me to voice my solidarity with the weak and defenseless who *cry out to God for help, for justice, for respect for their God-given dignity as human beings, for their basic human rights, for the freedom to believe and practice their faith* without fear or discrimination.... Today, in the Sudan, the Bishop of Rome, the Successor of Peter, repeats these words and encourages you to stand firm and to take heart. *The Lord is close to you. He will never leave you alone. The whole Church understands your distress and prays for you.*[2]

Fifteen years later, the crisis has only intensified. It seems clear that Pope Benedict wants to repeat that message. Significantly, he does it in the context of this important document on hope.

Reflection Questions

1. Pope Benedict speaks of hope as "a distinguishing mark of Christians." What does this mean in practical, real-life terms?

2. How do you see nihilism expressed in the culture and lives of the people around you?

3. How do you see hope, the kind of hope that St. Josephine Bakhita had, expressed in our culture or in the lives of people around you?

Prayer Prompts

1. Spend time in prayer with the key Scripture passages offered by the Pope in this section: Hebrews 10:22–23, First Thessalonians 4:13, Ephesians 2:12, and First Peter 3:15. On separate occasions, approach the passages slowly, without expecting any particular return for your time. Simply sit quietly with the words, and allow God to speak to you through them.

2. Spend some prayer time with St. Josephine Bakhita. As she is our elder sister in faith, certainly we can go to her with any concern or need. And the people of her native Sudan unquestionably deserve prayers of intercession from us while we're talking to her. But perhaps in the context of our study of this encyclical, it might be particularly important to ask her to help us face the most painful aspects of our own lives and to open ourselves ever more widely to God's gift of hope. St. Josephine, Universal Sister, Woman of Hope, pray for us! (My book, *Saints for Our Times: New Novenas and Prayers*[3] includes

an original novena to St. Josephine Bakhita, along with other material related to her.)

3. Pray for the people of Darfur.

4. Pray the prayer of the early Christians: Come, Lord Jesus!

Putting It into Practice

Real hope demands that we work on behalf of this world and its people, especially those in the most desperate situations. Consider what you can do to help them. To learn how you can help the people of Darfur, visit www.savedarfur.org (which represents a coalition of religious and humanitarian organizations) or www.crs.org (Catholic Relief Services) on the Web.

~~

The Concept of Faith-Based Hope in the New Testament and the Early Church

Can it change our lives? The Pope opens this section with this question. He repeats it several times in various ways throughout this document. In fact, we could say that the point of the entire document is to explain what an incredible difference the virtue of hope makes to our daily living—the hope that might otherwise seem harmless, quaint, and ultimately irrelevant to "real life" in the modern world.

Keep this in mind because this section of *Spe Salvi* might seem intimidating. Here Benedict the professor comes to the fore. He's standing at the chalkboard neatly writing some foreign words that he'd like us to consider for a moment. In fact, there's some Greek, Latin, *and* German! He also mentions some important folks from history to illustrate his points. Some famous saints and theologians show up, such as Francis of Assisi, Thomas Aquinas, and Gregory Nazianzen. But a few other colorful figures also appear, some of whom might be less familiar: Spartacus, Barabbas, and Bar-Kochba.

Benedict asks: Can hope change our lives? He answers with a resounding yes, and in this section, he begins to explain why. So struggling a bit with the words and our teacher's explanations will be well worth the effort.

Jesus Was Not Spartacus

Benedict begins by making clear what that yes mentioned above does *not* mean. Jesus, he says, was not Spartacus.

Spartacus was a slave, trained as a gladiator, in the Roman Republic (which would later become the Roman Empire) at the beginning of the first century B.C. He led a massive and violent revolt by an army of more than 100,000 slaves. His effort ultimately failed, but not before he scored some crushing military victories against the Roman army. History remembers Spartacus as a brilliant military tactician and violent revolutionary; other violent revolutionaries, including Karl Marx and Che Guevara, have used him as a model.

The Pope also comments that Jesus "was not engaged in a fight for political liberation like Barabbas or Bar-Kochba" (no. 4). Like Spartacus, these two men used violence in attempts to overthrow unjust and repressive political systems.

Barabbas makes a brief but important appearance in the Gospels, when Pilate offers the crowd the choice between him and Jesus for release at Passover. The Gospel of Mark says that Barabbas had been "in prison along with the rebels who had committed murder in a rebellion" (15:7). The rebellion would have been against the Roman Empire, which ruled Judea at the time, and Barabbas was probably a local hero, which explains the Jews' choice in his favor.

A century later, Bar-Kochba led a revolt against the same Roman Empire, also on behalf of the Jews. He was the ruthless leader of a three-year struggle that pitted 400,000 Jewish rebels against the armies of the Roman emperor Hadrian. In the end, Hadrian crushed the revolt and enacted even harsher measures against the Jews than had existed before.

The Pope's point, then, is clear. While Christian hope and faith have changed things and have had a massive impact on individual lives, on societies, and on history itself, the change is (he says more than once) "from within."

This marvelous changing of people and nations has marked the life of the Church along every step of her journey through history. But some Christians, having forgotten that change must always come from within, have tried to force it "from the outside." Such attempts have always led to tragedies and abuses. As Pope John Paul II used to insist, we must always seek to *propose* the Gospel to others, never *impose* it upon them.

A Fossilized Faith?

Most folks, though, rarely struggle with the temptation to become a modern-day Spartacus, changing the world by force and violence. The next danger the Pope addresses is one that we do face daily, and it's all the more dangerous if we don't realize it.

Pope Benedict reminds us that the religion of the Roman Empire, into which the Christian faith was born, had become "fossilized." Its people continued to carry out their religious rituals and traditions, but their worldview "had confined the gods to the realm of unreality." His words could be applied to many people in our own day, even among those who call themselves Christian.

One often hears about what a uniquely religious nation America is. A vast majority of us identify ourselves as religious, and more of us attend church regularly than our Christian brothers and sisters in Europe. But how seriously do we take our creeds? And what impact do they have on our lives?

As one who has worked in Catholic education and youth ministry for many years, I find it unsettling that few students today bother to argue about the existence of God. It seems to be an unimportant question to most of them. Talk of God, or his Church, or his sacraments is no more or less meaningful or provocative than talking about Allah, Zeus, or the mighty Thor. To many students, it all seems to have little to do with reality.

A related aspect of the religion of the Roman Empire at the birth of Christianity is also worth some consideration. Benedict speaks of the idea that the world was guided by "the elemental spirits of the universe" and "divine cosmic forces." But Christian faith meant rejecting this thinking, because it revealed that at the heart of everything is a personal God, a God of reason and love. Hence the Church's rejection, then and now, of astrology. How can anyone who has a relationship with the living God, walking together with him into the future, ever take seriously the astrological predictions that are found in so many newspapers and magazines?

Jesus the Philosopher

To understand rightly the kind of change Jesus brings, the Pope offers the ancient Christian image of Jesus as a philosopher. For many people today, the word suggests a scholar sitting in an ivory tower and thinking about airy ideas far removed from the realities of everyday life. As the Pope points out well, this is very different, almost the opposite in some ways, from what the Christians of the third and fourth centuries had in mind when they carved this image of Jesus onto their tombs

To them, a philosopher was "one who knew the art of being authentically human, the art of living and dying." He was a "teacher of life" who could "point out the path of life." They depicted Christ as philosopher by putting in one of his hands a Gospel book, the written treasury of the life and teachings of the Teacher of life. In the other hand appears a traveling staff, because he does not sit aloof from "real life" but rather walked a real human life—with all the struggles and demands that entails—and still walks with each of us along the paths of our own lives.

This image is reflected in the Second Vatican Council's teaching about Jesus, which Pope John Paul II embraced and developed enthusiastically. Neither the Council nor the late Pope used the philosopher image, but both present Jesus as God's revelation of what it truly means to be human.

The other Christ-image that Benedict presents is the shepherd, who represents the longing for "the tranquil and simple life," and who guides and accompanies each of us, even unto death. For an illustration of this early Christian image, we need look no further than the *Catechism of the Catholic Church*. The image on the cover is a logo that the Vatican insists must be printed by all publishers of the *Catechism* worldwide. Flip to the copyright page to see the explanation for this choice of

images. (It's no coincidence, surely, that Benedict, who proposes the image again in *Spe Salvi*, was also the cardinal who
presided over the entire process of the *Catechism's* compilation
and publication!)

We shouldn't pass over Benedict's beautiful comments on
the image without pausing to reflect on them:

> The true shepherd is the one who knows even the path
> that passes through the valley of death; one who walks
> with me even on the path of final solitude, where no one
> can accompany me, guiding me through: he himself has
> walked this path, he has descended into the kingdom of
> death, he has conquered death, and he has returned to
> accompany us now and to give us the certainty that,
> together with him, we can find a way through. The real-
> ization that there is One who even in death accompanies
> me, and with his "rod and his staff comforts me," so that
> "I fear no evil," (cf. Ps 23 [22]:4)—this was the new "hope"
> that arose over the life of believers. (no. 6)[4]

Greek to Me

Then things get a little more technical. For good reason,
some have suggested that a good editor might have been helpful here. Let's see if we can clarify things a bit.

Benedict returns to the Letter to the Hebrews. He wants to
draw our attention now to a few words, and one in particular,
because of what they say about real hope. In chapter 10, the
author of Hebrews presents the death of Jesus on the cross as
the fulfillment and completion of all Old Testament sacrifices
and also as a call for us to persevere in faith. This leads us to
the famous definition of faith in chapter 11, verse 1: "Faith is

the realization of what is hoped for and evidence of things not seen."[5]

Of course, the Letter to the Hebrews, like the rest of the New Testament, was originally written in Greek, not English. And the Holy Spirit's gift of biblical inspiration applied to the original authors of the Bible, not to later translators. (In fact, Benedict does not flinch from criticizing a translation currently approved for use by Catholics in his native Germany.)

Where you see the word *realization* in the text I present, the original Greek word is *hypostasis*. Realization suggests that something (what we hope for) is being made real by our faith. With faith comes the reality of what we hope for, already made present and effective in us.[6]

However, in recent centuries, the word has sometimes been translated in a way that loses a lot of the meaning Benedict says it's intended to have. Martin Luther understood *hypostasis* as an assurance, a strong expectation of something that will one day be received. Rather than saying something about what faith *really is* and *really does*, it's about an individual believer's *attitude about faith*. (For example, the *New International Version* renders Hebrews 11:1 as: "Now faith is being sure of what we hope for and certain of what we do not see.")

In turn, the meaning we give to *hypostasis* affects how we understand another word in the same sentence: *elenchos*. It's translated as "evidence" in the *New American Bible*. Benedict suggests *proof* as well. Both are more objective than the idea of a *conviction* that is sometimes offered.

This is more than quibbling about an obscure Greek word. It affects what we understand faith to be and what it does in us. Benedict insists that faith is not just really wanting the fulfillment of God's promises and feeling confident about one day getting it. By our faith, what we hope for is ~~made real~~ in us now.

Reflection Questions

1. "Can Christian hope change our lives?" The Pope insists on pressing the question. What if someone posed it to you? What can you take from what you've read so far to help answer that question?

2. What's the difference between Jesus and Spartacus? Why is the difference important? What if Jesus had been more like Spartacus?

3. What impact might the Pope's reflection in this section have on the way you look at and move toward your own death?

Prayer Prompts

1. Spend time in prayer contemplating the image of Christ the true philosopher, who shows us the way to be truly human, the way beyond death. Don't just think about him, but spend time *with him*, the One who reveals to you your most authentic self.

2. Spend time, too, with Christ the shepherd. Know his protective presence and attentive guidance. Thank him for being with you, even—and especially—in "the valley of the shadow of death." Sitting with him, pray Psalm 23.

3. Benedict's comments about the nature of faith in Hebrews 11:1, and the translation of that verse, can seem a bit academic. So it doesn't remain only an academic matter, reflect

prayerfully on the verse. Give thanks to God for the gift of faith that truly does make God's promises real and effective in us. Ask him to open your heart ever more receptively to the gift.

Putting It into Practice

What aspect of society (your community, nation, or world) do you recognize as needing change, the kind of change that deeper faith would help bring about? In what ways can you begin to help nourish such change by fostering that kind of faith? A more consistent personal witness? A letter to the editor? Participation in a parish-based ministry?

Eternal Life: What Is It?

The Pope will not let go of the question about what hope really means and the difference it makes in "real life." Here it is again as he opens this next section of his letter: "Is the Christian faith also for us today a life-changing and life-sustaining hope?" (no. 10). Though this Pope is a world-class theologian, his insistence on a careful answer to this singular question shows that he writes with a pastor's heart. He is writing not simply with an audience of theologians and bishops in mind, but for people who face the ongoing struggles of everyday living.

The Source of Our Struggles

The struggles of everyday living have everything to do with his comments in this section about eternal life and the desire for it planted in all our hearts: "Ultimately we want only one thing—'the blessed life,' the life which is simply life, simply 'happiness.' In the final analysis, there is nothing else that we ask for in prayer. Our journey has no other goal—it is about this alone" (no. 11).

All of us experience this yearning, but many fail to realize what our hearts seek. Like a hungry toddler who tries to eat a crayon, we reach for things that can never fill us—and can even kill us. The Pope puts it this way:

> In some way we want life itself, true life, untouched even by death; yet at the same time we do not know the thing towards which we feel driven. We cannot stop reaching out for it, and yet we know that all we can experience or accomplish is not what we yearn for. This unknown "thing" is the true "hope" which drives us, and at the same time the fact that it is unknown is the cause of all forms of despair and also of all efforts, whether positive or destructive, directed towards worldly authenticity and human authenticity. (no. 12)

Certainly that's been true of people of all times and places. But we live in a time when people enjoy more options than ever before, and these seem more satisfying than ever before. Yet they can be more destructive to our lives than ever before. That's a dangerous mix! It doesn't take a theologian to recognize the vast fallout of so many of these choices—broken families, fatherless or motherless children, poverty, addiction, disease, depression, anger, and so on. These are not hidden effects, but many people don't or aren't willing to acknowledge the clear connection between the choices and the consequences.

What does Christian faith have to offer?

A Faith That Does Something

For the second time in his letter, Pope Benedict speaks of the "performative" (rather than simply "informative") nature of

Christian faith. He means that Christianity is not simply a collection of information, even crucially important information. It's not about simply knowing what the Creed says, like the dates and names we learn in a history class.

For example, if I understand world history better than most other people, I may have a clearer sense of what came before us and how we got to where we are today. But it's unlikely that this knowledge will change my life in any qualitative way (unless I hope to be a history teacher). But, says the Pope, "knowing" the Good News—hearing it proclaimed, understanding it, and accepting it in faith—*does* change us. It is, he says, "a message which shapes our life in a new way."

How? There are many ways, but Pope Benedict has one particular way in mind because it has everything to do with hope. He brings up the topic of Baptism, because the baptismal liturgy draws out the faith-eternal life connection very clearly in the dialogue between priest and parents the Pope describes for us. The liturgy itself teaches us: *With faith comes eternal life.*

"But then the question arises, do we really want this?" Benedict's question will surprise some readers. If we've been fortunate enough to have been raised and to live within a Christian environment, we might well ask, "Who would *not* want eternal life?"

Benedict has been a keen observer of Western society for many years, and he now carries pastoral responsibility for the Church throughout the world. He knows that many people today will not welcome the idea of eternal life because they do not possess an understanding of its true meaning.

Let me explain. Say the word "pasta" to a person who has grown up thoroughly immersed in an Italian culture, and it carries a wide range of connotations, varieties, and levels of meaning. Pasta comes in dozens of shapes and sizes, and pasta sauces come in even more varieties. Some types of pasta just go better with certain kinds of sauces. *Amatriciana* (a light and slightly spicy tomato sauce with bits of a type of bacon called pancetta) could easily be put on any kind of pasta, but it is most often served with *bucatini* (which is a lot like spaghetti, only thicker and with a tiny hole running down the entire length of the tube).

Say pasta to most twenty-first-century Americans, and they think almost exclusively of spaghetti with a thick tomato sauce and a meatball on the side.

Benedict, familiar with the post-Christian culture around us, realizes that many people will not automatically welcome the idea of eternal life as a wonderful concept. That idea once carried with it a whole array of images and concepts that we can no longer presume. Today, many people simply think of it as life as we now know it going on forever.

An Inadequate Term

Certainly there would be some good things about life as we know it for eternity. Our life is not all bad. But an endless life on earth would bring plenty of trouble as well. The frustrations, pain, difficulties, struggles, insecurity, fragility, loneliness, and discontentment of this life would go on forever, too. That kind of eternal life, the Pope says, truly would be "more a curse than a gift … monotonous and ultimately unbearable."

Besides, these troublesome aspects of life are doled out unequally among people. For some, life is mostly comfortable and pleasant, while for others it brings constant misery, so this "eternal life" would be a more attractive prospect for some people more than others.

But this is not what Christians mean in speaking of eternal life. What we have in mind is neither simply *eternal*, as we normally use the word, nor simply *life*, as we normally use that word! The Pope is blunt: "Inevitably, it is an inadequate term that creates confusion."

And yet, to clarify what we *do* mean is no easy task. Even the rigorous and deliberative mind of Benedict, the same mind that insisted on careful consideration of the nuanced meanings of Greek vocabulary just a few pages before, slips into what is closer to poetry than prose in trying to describe the concept.

> [E]ternity is not an unending succession of days in the calendar, but something more like the supreme moment of satisfaction, in which totality embraces us and we embrace totality.... It would be like plunging into the ocean of infinite love, a moment in which time—the before and after—no longer exists. We can only attempt to grasp the

The Pope and St. Augustine

○ Young Joseph Ratzinger's doctoral dissertation topic was "The People of God and the House of God in the Teaching of Augustine About the Church."

○ Pope Benedict visited the tomb of St. Augustine in April 2007, calling him a "model of conversion" for all Christians.

○ The shell in the Pope's coat of arms refers to St. Augustine's story of a boy on the seashore who taught him about the impossibility of fully understanding the Holy Trinity.

○ In *Spe Salvi,* St. Augustine is mentioned nine times (more than any other person).

idea that such a moment is life in the full sense, a plunging ever anew into the vastness of being, in which we are simply overwhelmed with joy. (no. 12)

Eternal life is a state of being, not a place. It is a reality that we can begin to encounter, if only in shadows and hints, even now in this life, and into which we will one day be swept completely. That is where Christian hope ultimately lies.

Reflection Questions

1. What is the difference between living forever and eternal life?

2. Do the Pope's reflections change your image of heaven, or your ideas about it? If so, how?

3. Think about popular images of heaven. How are they helpful to understanding what the Pope is saying? How are they less than helpful?

Prayer Prompts

1. Ask God to make you more aware of the eternal life he has given to you even now.

2. John 6 makes it clear that eternal life is closely connected with eating and drinking the Body and Blood of Christ. Bring that chapter of John's Gospel into your prayer time. Keep it prayerfully in mind the next time you receive Holy Communion, and give thanks for the gift of eternal life you have received.

Putting It into Practice

Find out the day you were baptized and mark it on your calendar as a day of celebrating the gift of eternal life. (Do the same for your children if you have young ones in the house.)

———— ❧ ————

Is Christian Hope Individualistic?

When Joseph Ratzinger—world-class theologian and now Pope—says that reading a particular book played a crucial part in his understanding of the Christian faith, we might want to take note. That's exactly what then-Cardinal Ratzinger wrote in 1989 when he penned the foreword to a new English edition of Henri de Lubac's *Catholicism: Christ and the Common Destiny of Man.* Two decades later, as Pope, he is pointing to the book again, this time in an encyclical.

Who is Henri de Lubac? What makes this book so special? And what does it have to do with Christian hope?

Returning to the Sources

In the first decades of the twentieth century, an important renewal in several key fields of Catholic theology began to take shape, especially in liturgy, Scripture, and ecclesiology (theological study of the Church). Henri de Lubac, a Jesuit, was one of several bright young theologians in Europe who began to explore some fascinating aspects of the Church's theological heritage that had been mostly forgotten for quite a few centuries.[7] They called their basic project *ressourcement* (French for "return to the sources"). But they were not simply unearthing archaic theological ideas; they believed the ideas could revitalize the Church in the modern world. Other theologians associated with this work were the French Dominicans Yves Congar and Marie-Dominique Chenu, and the German theologians Joseph Ratzinger and Karl Rahner, a Jesuit.

The story of these theologians is now familiar: Half a century after a Church-wide crackdown on a heresy called modernism, the ecclesiastical culture of the 1940s and 1950s still viewed with suspicion anything that even resembled it. Many theologians experienced the distrust of others within the Church, and a few, de Lubac and Congar most notably, were forbidden for a time to teach Catholic theology. Their obedient and patient acceptance of such measures testifies to their virtue and integrity. Eventually, much of their work came to be widely accepted; they were very influential in the work of the Second Vatican Council. Several of them were later named cardinals by Popes Paul VI and John Paul II. Ratzinger, of course, is now Pope Benedict XVI.

With this as background, we can now ask: What problem was de Lubac addressing in his book *Catholicism*, and why does Benedict bring it up here?

To Hell with the World?

As in the previous section of *Spe Salvi*, Benedict presents his reflections in answer to a question. Here he asks, "Is

Christian hope individualistic?" He believes that a casual observer might be forgiven for answering with a confident yes. That's because too many Christians have lived as though it were so, treating their faith as (in Benedict's words) "a way of abandoning the world to its misery and taking refuge in a private form of eternal salvation" (no. 13).

In other words: *The world's going to hell in a handbasket, but the world pretty much deserves it anyway. Just let me say my prayers and get my Communion. What the world does, or where it goes, is not my concern. My job is to save my own soul.*

Throughout the nineteenth century and well into the twentieth this attitude was common among many Catholics. (To be fair, "the world" was sometimes an unwelcoming place for a faithful Catholic to be living in, too.) Then along came Henri de Lubac and his 1947 book, *Catholicism: Christ and the Common Destiny of Man* (the original French subtitle translates as "The Social Aspects of Dogma").

In this book, de Lubac confronted an excessively individualistic idea of Christian faith with a massive amount of evidence that the early Church saw things quite differently. De Lubac showed that in its essence the Gospel is all about the interconnectedness and unity of humanity, and that we cannot live out the Gospel while ignoring that truth. He demonstrated that this idea was (as Ratzinger put it in his 1989 foreword) an essential part of the Christian faith—not merely one idea among many (like one room in a large house), but the foundation of it all.

The Social Character of Hope

So Pope Benedict insists now that when we speak about what our hope means, we can never forget its "social character." My Christian hope can never be something exclusively about me, God's presence to me, and my personal relationship with him. If it's only about saving my own soul, it's not an authentically Christian faith or hope.

My hope, and the life it brings me, "is linked to a lived union with a 'people,' and for each individual it can only be attained with this 'we.' It presupposes that we escape from the prison of our 'I,' because only in the openness of this universal subject does our gaze open out to the source of joy, to love itself—to God" (no. 14).

In practical terms, this means that our hope always calls us to "the building up of this world" (no. 15). Concern for the world around us and the people that fill it is a non-negotiable part of being a Catholic Christian. Put into more specific and concrete terms, this means that issues such as human rights, world peace, concern for the poor, health care, marriage and family life, and the evangelization of our culture must all be "on the radar" for each of us.

Benedict's example from the life and words of St. Bernard of Clairvaux is a reminder that everyone, whatever their Christian vocation, is called to live and work for the good of others. Even cloistered monks and nuns today, as in St. Bernard's time, are called, in a specific way, to live and work on behalf of the world and the people in it.

There is a monastery of cloistered Carmelite nuns that I sometimes visit, usually to ask for prayers for particular needs or situations. I stand on one side of their little curtained screen and the sister who greets me stands on the other. We talk about the world and my family and their community. Having visited many times, I have a sense that most of the nuns there would object to any suggestion that they are somehow "hiding" from the world, because they have the world very much in their hearts and their daily prayers. We will never know, this side of heaven, the impact of those prayers on each of our lives.

St. Bernard of Clairvaux

- 1090–1153
- Cistercian abbot
- Mystic, theologian, adviser to kings and popes
- Doctor of the Church

If this "community-oriented vision," as *Spe Salvi* calls it, does not seem like such a startling new insight to attentive Catholics today and if we can easily see evidence of this very idea widely accepted and practiced throughout the Church today, we have to thank Father de Lubac. (This was surely a major reason why Pope John Paul II named him a cardinal in 1983.)

Reflection Questions

1. Have you fallen prey to the temptation to make your faith and your hope solely a private, personal matter? If so, in what way?

2. In what ways have you succeeded in connecting your faith and hope to the world and to the people around you?

3. Pope Benedict concludes this section by asking, "Are we not perhaps seeing once again, in the light of current history,

that no positive world order can prosper where souls are over-grown?" (no. 15). What does he mean by an "overgrowing of souls," and what evidence of it do you see in our world today?

Prayer Prompts

1. Think about the Pope's example of the life and words of St. Bernard on our responsibility for the world. Consider that one way of helping the world is to pray for and on behalf of it. Begin to more consciously bring the world, with all its concerns and needs, to your prayer.

2. Next time you receive Communion, make yourself aware of the intense connection it provides with the Body of Christ, which is the Church on earth, with all of your brothers and sisters in Christ.

3. Allow this section to serve as an examination of conscience. Have I kept my faith too private a matter? Have I allowed my faith to form me into a person who serves others?

Putting It into Practice

We could put into practice the ideas Benedict presents in this section in many ways. No one could attempt all of them. But we all should be doing some of them, in some way. In what ways do you already contribute to making this world a better, more humane, more just, more pleasant place to live? How might you take one more step in that direction this week?

The Transformation of Christian Faith: Hope in the Modern Age

The Pope, this doctor of our souls, has diagnosed a disease within the spiritual life of Christians, one that distorts our idea of what hope truly is. Now he looks for its origin. Where did this just-save-my-own-soul disease come from? How did we "catch" it? He asks: "How could the idea have developed that Jesus' message is narrowly individualistic and aimed at each person singly?" (no. 16).

In exploring this question, we discover how closely our faith is intermeshed with the culture that surrounds it. Problems within the Church often reflect what is going on in the world.

Benedict's argument comes in three steps. To make them more understandable, I will offer some explanations and additional background information. It starts, he says, with a man named Bacon.

"The Great Restoration"

Francis Bacon (1561–1626) was born into a prominent British political family. A bright, well-liked man with a gift for public speaking, Bacon flourished as a politician. He held increasingly important governmental positions and was finally named lord chancellor of England at the age of fifty-seven (the same post held by St. Thomas More less than a century earlier).

But Bacon had too many talents and intellectual gifts to limit himself to politics. He threw himself into literature, science, and, most of all, philosophy, achieving incredible success in each of these fields.

His remarkable book *Essays* effectively created a whole new genre of English literature. His new approach to scientific research (which every junior high school student learns today as "the scientific method") laid the groundwork for countless developments and achievements for centuries. But his philosophy undergirded all of this.

Bacon developed a detailed outline for a massive philosophical-scientific project that he called the *Instauratio Magna* —the Great Reconstruction. Though some of this project was never completed before his death, one major part of it, the *Novum Organum* ("new instrument" or "tool"), was published in 1620. It has had a crucial impact on science, philosophy, and Western culture right up to our own day. The Pope sees Bacon's book as laying the very foundations of the modern age.

The title refers to the *Organon*, an influential collection of Aristotle's writings on logic. By using this title, Bacon claimed to offer a new beginning to human knowledge and understanding of the natural world, the likes of which had not been seen since Aristotle himself 2,000 years earlier. (Bacon was not troubled by low self-esteem!)

The *Novum Organum* claimed that old ways of thinking and reasoning, rooted in Aristotle and developed by the medieval philosophers who had basically built Western culture, had to be cast aside. Bacon asserted that their prejudices, speculations, and logical proofs by syllogism served to muddle and distort rather than help our understanding of the world.

"[S]trangled with the entrails of the last priest"

Bacon laid much of the groundwork for the Enlightenment, a philosophical movement based on the exultation of human reason. Reason alone, it said, could be considered a trustworthy source for understanding the universe. Dogma, tradition, and authority were nothing but superstition, not sources of knowledge. Enlightenment philosophers disdained the very idea of a divine revelation that could not be known by our ability to reason. They also scorned the authority that had for centuries protected and passed on this revelation. Enlightenment meant freedom from the influence of any such authority.

You don't need a philosophy degree to figure out that for most people who embraced Enlightenment ideas, this meant that the Church was an enemy. And you don't need to be a sage to recognize the continued influence of Enlightenment ideas today.

Benedict has this outlook in mind when he writes:

The kingdom of reason, in fact, is expected as the new condition of the human race once it has attained total freedom. The political conditions of such a kingdom of reason and freedom, however, appear at first sight somewhat ill defined. Reason and freedom seem to guarantee by themselves, by virtue of their intrinsic goodness, a new and perfect human community. The two key concepts of "reason" and "freedom," however, were tacitly interpreted as being in conflict with the shackles of faith and of the Church as well as those of the political structures of the period. Both concepts therefore contain a revolutionary potential of enormous explosive force. (no. 18)

The Enlightenment was not all bad, however, and some truly good fruits grew out of it. One of the greatest of these was a dramatic development in the Western world's appreciation of human dignity and human rights. One of the most important writings from this time, for example, is the United States Declaration of Independence, which champions human rights. The Church has welcomed and even embraced this development enthusiastically. The great Pope John Paul II, for example, made the defense of human rights a key aspect of his teaching throughout his long pontificate.

But the Enlightenment's heightened appreciation of the value of reason came with a belligerence toward faith, revelation, and authority. A quote attributed to the French writer Denis Diderot says: "Man will never be free until the last king is strangled with the entrails of the last priest." In a most frightening way, these words came to life during the French Revolution.

In 1789, Enlightenment ideas burst out violently in what had previously been the most Catholic country on earth. Following a tumultuous meeting of the Estates General, a general assembly that had not met in more than a century, an angry mob attacked the Bastille fortress, a symbol of France's monarchy. This event unleashed a bloody, fanatical revolution that would last six years, during which 250,000 people were arrested and almost 30,000 people (many thousands of whom never received a trial of any kind) executed by guillotine.

Leaders insisted on completely eliminating from French society both the monarchy and the Church, using the most horrendous means to achieve these ends. The history is a long and complicated one, but a list of a few significant dates and events will paint a general picture:

Oct. 6, 1789:   King Louis XVI is forcibly removed from power.

Oct. 28, 1789:   An official "provisional suspension" of all religious vows is proclaimed.

Feb. 13, 1790:   The suspension of religious vows is made permanent.

Apr. 6, 1792:   The government announces the suppression of religious orders and the wearing of religious habits.

Apr. 8, 1792:   Easter Masses are interrupted by mobs, and churches are plundered.

Aug. 17, 1792:   All religious houses are ordered to be vacated.

Dec. 25, 1792:   Not a single church bell rings in Paris to mark the celebration of Christmas.

Jan. 21, 1793:   King Louis XVI is executed before a cheering crowd of thousands in Paris.

Sept. 2, 1793:   The Reign of Terror begins (a period of ruthless violence lasting almost a year).

Oct. 5, 1793:   The seven-day Judeo-Christian week is officially abolished, and "Day One of Year One" is marked as September 22, 1792, which was the first equinox after the fall of the monarchy.

Oct. 16, 1793: Queen Marie Antoinette is executed.

Nov. 10, 1793: The Cathedral of Notre Dame is re-named the "Temple of Reason" and this day is celebrated as "the Feast of Reason."

Jun. 10, 1794: The six-week "Red Terror," an even more intensely violent time, begins; 1,400 people are guillotined in Paris between this date and July 27.

Jul. 17, 1794: The sixteen Carmelite nuns of Compiegne are executed.

Jul. 28, 1794: Maximilien Robespierre, previously a prominent Revolution leader, is executed.

Jul. 29, 1794: The mayor of Paris and eighty-seven members of the city council are guillotined as Robespierre's accomplices.[8]

Rarely has so much violence been carried out in the name of civilized society.

Communist Revolution

As he traces the development of the modern view of life and of the entire universe, Pope Benedict wants to make one more stop in his survey of history. He brings us to another revolution. While Russia's Communist Revolution did not take place until 1917, it was the flowering of the work of two men who lived two generations earlier.

To "get it," we have to be aware of yet another revolution. Until the end of the 1700s, people lived on what they grew and built by themselves. Then machines began to change everything about business, the economy, and everyday life in the United States and Europe. Suddenly, a few people running machines could produce the same amount it would once have taken hundreds of individuals to produce. Gather lots of machines into large buildings, hire a workforce to run them, and you have a factory. The Industrial Revolution had begun.

All of this brought some positive (and positively astonishing) developments and changes to everyday life. Lots of work got done more quickly and effectively. Many products and conveniences—the automobile, locomotive, steel, photography, and countless others—were widely available to people who previously could never have dreamed of such things.

But all this also brought a new set of problems, some of them tragic. People soon realized that these new machines could multiply profits. Factory owners exploited their workers, forcing them to labor in unsafe and unsanitary environments for little pay. Though child labor had existed before (children commonly worked on family farms), with the Industrial Revolution, children themselves became less important than the work they did, the machines they served, and the money they made for factory owners. (In 1802, a law had to be passed in Britain, prohibiting children under nine years of age from working and limiting workdays to twelve hours for older children.) Factory jobs in cities meant shifting populations, and city living conditions became filthy and dangerous.

One radical solution to these problems came from the pen of the writer Friedrich Engels, whose ideas were taken up and put into action by his friend Karl Marx. Both men were from Prussia. (In *Spe Salvi*, Benedict refers to Engels' alarming description of British society in 1845.) The most just solution that Engels and Marx could envision was socialism—a society in which class distinctions disappeared because factories, railroads, and land (all means of production and distribution) would be owned not by individuals but by society as a whole. Although socialist ideas were not new at all (Plato wrote about them in the fourth century B.C., and, among Catholic thinkers, St. Thomas More, in the sixteenth century), Engels and Marx put a new spin on them, calling this approach Communism.

While many thinkers had assumed that socialism would be agreed upon by all sectors of a society, the two Prussians believed this was impossible. No meaningful change would ever willingly be accepted by leaders of business, who had the most to lose by it. As Marx saw it, if the Industrial Revolution taught us anything, it was that history is a constant struggle among economic groups, each maintaining its own comfort and success by dominating and exploiting the others. The only way for a more just system to be born was for society's workers to force it upon business owners. "Workers of the world, unite!" was the rallying cry, the final words of Marx's famous *Communist Manifesto* of 1848.

Marx and Engels did not live to see their thinking bear fruit, but it became increasingly popular years after they died. In October 1917, it exploded onto the stage of history.

In February that year, Russia's czarist government had been overthrown. Vladimir Lenin, a vocal advocate of Marxism, took advantage of the chaos to call for a Communist Russia. He demanded complete restructuring of society, with power put in the hands of the "soviets," local governing councils elected by the commoners. He quickly gained widespread support, and on October 25 troops supporting Lenin's Bolshevik party (known as the Red Army) took over government buildings in Russia's capital. In the following days, all private land and Church-owned property were seized, and private bank accounts were confiscated.

Many opposed the Bolsheviks, both in and outside of Russia. This led to a massive and bloody civil war that lasted from 1918 to 1922 and resulted in the establishment of the Union of Soviet Socialist Republics (U.S.S.R.).

For sixty-seven years, the Soviet government maintained Marxist Communism as a way of life in the U.S.S.R. and tried to spread it around the globe. But the people of the Soviet Union and the nations that fell under its control paid a bitter price. Communist authorities maintained control only through harsh repression of the people, which cost millions of lives. The era of Joseph Stalin stands out as an especially tragic period.

Progress Is Not Progress Without an Ethical Element

Undoubtedly there are positive elements to every one of these pivotal moments of modern history, as I've tried to suggest. But they also bear witness to what, in this section of *Spe Salvi*, Benedict calls "the ambiguity of progress" These historical moments clearly illustrate the lesson he draws: "If technical progress is not matched by corresponding progress in man's ethical formation, in man's inner growth ([see] Eph 3:16; 2 Cor 4:16), then it is not progress at all, but a threat for man and for the world" (no. 22). The Pope cites the twentieth-century philosopher Theodor Adorno's dramatic words: "[P]rogress, seen accurately, is progress from the sling to the atom bomb."

Without keeping our bearings through close attention to ethics, human society gets trapped in a dangerous spiral. We are constantly pushing ahead to do everything we find ourselves able to do, without ever asking whether we *should* be doing it.

We are, the Pope says, "urgently in need of integration through reason's openness to the saving forces of faith, to the differentiation between good and evil.... Reason therefore needs faith if it is to be completely itself: reason and faith need one another in order to fulfill their true nature and their mission" (no. 23).

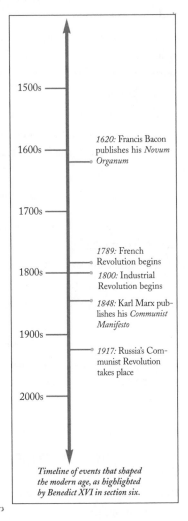

1500s ——

1600s —— *1620:* Francis Bacon publishes his *Novum Organum*

1700s ——

1789: French Revolution begins
1800s —— *1800:* Industrial Revolution begins

1848: Karl Marx publishes his *Communist Manifesto*
1900s ——

1917: Russia's Communist Revolution takes place

2000s ——

Timeline of events that shaped the modern age, as highlighted by Benedict XVI in section six.

Reflection Questions

1. In what ways did Marx and Engels get it right? What did they get wrong?

2. If you're old enough to remember it, what are your memories of the historic political changes that took place in 1989, with the fall of the Berlin Wall and the dissolution of the Soviet Union?

3. Adorno mentioned the atom bomb as an example of how progress can become a threat to humanity. What other examples of this do you see in today's world?

Prayer Prompts

1. Pray for people of science and technology, that they may never become caught up in the blind pursuit of "progress," but be guided by an awareness of what is right and good.

2. Reflect on the two Scripture passages (Eph 3:16 and 2 Cor 4:16) that the Pope cites in the last sentence of number 22.

3. With an eye on the sad episodes of human history, one can only pray for all people and leaders of our own day. "Guide and protect us, Lord, along our path into the future."

Putting It into Practice

Identify ways that you put "progress" (your paycheck? position at work? success in school?) before people, and take steps today to make your life a statement that people and their dignity are more important.

The True Shape of Christian Hope

That last section was a challenging one. It was, in fact, classic Joseph Ratzinger—a careful combination of demanding scholarly investigation (the professor) and faith-nourishing reflection (the pastor). But take heart. What follows will be enriching and often beautiful but won't call for quite as great a strain on the brain.

Having shown us where we've gone off track in understanding and living the virtue of hope, Pope Benedict now wants to paint a picture of what real hope looks like. Here is the heart of *Spe Salvi*. All of the Pope's reflections up to now have been leading us to this section, and all that comes after it will be drawing out what he says here.

"The moral well-being of the world"

Readers who are old enough will remember how momentous it was to watch news reports in 1989 about the Berlin Wall literally being torn down and the spectacular political changes that followed. The Cold War had dragged on for roughly half a century, causing tremendous international tension (and anxiety for anyone who had sense enough to realize its dangers). It ended as the Soviet Union collapsed. Even our maps had to be updated, and the nation that President Reagan had called "the evil empire" no longer appeared on them.

At the beginning of the '90s, politicians or commentators would often speak of a "new world order" in tones of awe and excitement. One could easily get the impression that after a tragic twentieth century—World War I, Hitler, World War II, Stalin, the Cold War—we could now turn the page of history and look forward to a bright and satisfying future.

For about a decade, it almost seemed true. The world still had its problems, such as ethnic wars in Eastern Europe and the tragic slaughter in Rwanda, but at least these regional conflicts did not erupt into worldwide wars as we had experienced before. Since September 2001, however, we've all been more painfully aware that the "world order" may be new, but it's no more free of major conflicts, problems, and tragedies than the old one.

That utopian expectation at the end of the twentieth century was not new. The remarkable progress in our scientific knowledge and technical abilities following Bacon's *Novum Organum* has led many people—including some of the most influential scientists and philosophers—to expect a sort of golden age in human history, when all will live in peace and our struggles and failures will be a thing of the past.

In the opening paragraphs of this section, the Pope insists that such an expectation was, is, and always will be naïve. Despite "continuous progress toward an ever greater mastery of nature ... in the field of ethical awareness and more deci-sion-making, there is no similar possibility of accumulation for the simple reason that man's freedom is always new and he must always make his decisions anew" (no. 24).

Consider the matter on a small scale. As I have gone through life, I've had my moral failures. I have often learned from these mistakes, and sometimes (though not as often as I wish) my later choices have become better as a result of what I have learned. My children can learn a bit from the mistakes that I have made, if I'm willing to teach them and they're will-ing to learn. But that learning is not an automatic inheritance in the way that technological progress and scientific knowledge are. (I had no access to cell phones or the Internet when I was a teenager; they certainly do.) Ultimately, they will make their own moral choices, and sometimes they will make the very same mistakes I made decades earlier (and their grandparents made long before that). Other mistakes will be all their own. They will learn from the mistakes they make, I hope, and someday their own children will make them, too! It's as true among peoples and nations as it is in families. Says the Pope:

> Since man always remains free and since his freedom is always fragile, the kingdom of good will never be definitively established in this world.... What this means is that every generation has the task of engaging anew in the arduous search for the right way to order human affairs; this task is never simply completed.... Francis Bacon and those who followed in the intellectual current of modernity that he inspired were wrong to believe that man would be redeemed through science. Such an expec-tation asks too much of science; this kind of hope is decep-tive. (nos. 24b–25)

That's not pessimistic; it's realistic. Notice that the Pope doesn't hesitate to direct some criticism at modern-day Christians as well:

> On the other hand, we must also acknowledge that modern Christianity, faced with the successes of science in progressively structuring the world, has to a large extent restricted its attention to the individual and his salvation. In doing so it has limited the horizon if its hope and has failed to recognize sufficiently the greatness of its task—even if it has continued to achieve great things in the formation of man and in care for the weak and the suffering. (no. 25)

Ouch. We have allowed the modern mindset to convince us that faith is a private matter and even irrelevant to society. We have swallowed the line that faith has nothing to offer to the world and that everyone is better off if we simply keep our faith to ourselves.

"Redeemed by love"

So while science and technology have benefited humanity in some almost breathtaking ways, they don't heal the wound at the very heart of our nature that makes us so susceptible to conflict, selfishness, greed, violence, and hunger for power. They can even serve these darker aspects of our nature. We have plenty of real-life examples; imaginary ones are not necessary.

Humanity, the Pope insists, "is redeemed by love." Numbers 26 and 27 of *Spe Salvi* include some of the most poignant and well-written passages of the encyclical. There's no need for a philosophy degree to get the drift of what he's saying here. Few people who have lived beyond childhood will fail to recognize the truth of the Pope's words: "When someone has the experience of a great love in his life, this is a moment of 'redemption' which gives new meaning to his life."

Many of us will think immediately of human love—our relationships with parents, children, spouses, or friends—as we consider these lines, and the Pope would be fine with that. But he pushes the point further. The love in human relationships "cannot by itself resolve the question of his life. It is love that remains fragile. It can be destroyed by death. The human being needs unconditional love.... If this absolute love exists, in its absolute certainty, then—only then—is man 'redeemed,' whatever should happen to him in his particular circumstances" (no. 26).

Here is love's connection to hope. *We gain a living and iron-clad sense of the goodness and meaning of our lives, even in the worst circumstances, not by clinging to dry, philosophical convictions, but by our experience of the love that is stronger than death!*

There is so much richness here, it's hard not to keep quoting the Pope: "Life in its true sense is not something we have exclusively in or from ourselves: it is a relationship. And life in its totality is a relationship with him who is the source of life. If we are in relation with him who does not die, who is Life itself and Love itself, then we are in life. Then we 'live'" (no. 27).

The Pope has placed love at the very center of the entire argument of *Spe Salvi*. If earlier he emphasized the unbreakable link between the virtues of hope and faith, he does the same here with hope and love. One who doesn't know God and his love "is ultimately without hope, without the great hope that sustains the whole of life."

Being for Others

But the Pope insists that we must not let these ideas lead us back to an individualistic understanding of Christian faith and life, reducing it to "God just loves me so much, isn't that wonderful?" Truly knowing God's love will always compel me to turn to others, who are just as much the focus of his love as I am. The Pope quotes St. Maximus to illustrate the bond between our communion with Christ and our responsibility to others. "Christ died for all," writes Benedict. "To live for him means allowing oneself to be drawn into his *being for others*" (no. 28).

St. Maximus the Confessor

○ 580–662

○ monk

○ wrote many works of spiritual theology

○ defended the dual wills (both human and divine) of Christ

○ tortured and then exiled until his death

Here the Pope offers his beloved St. Augustine as an example. St. Augustine was a scholarly man who by nature wanted to separate himself from the world and dedicate himself to private prayer and study, but he found that God asked more of him. Pope Benedict is humble enough not to mention the parallels with his own life. During the twenty-four years he worked as head of one of the Vatican's most important congregations, Cardinal Ratzinger had asked Pope John Paul II more than once for retirement, longing to spend the rest of his life studying and writing. The Pope told him he needed him where he was. When John Paul II died in 2005, Cardinal Ratzinger was seventy-eight years old and surely thought his moment to retire had finally arrived. But instead of retiring, he was elected Pope!

Reflection Questions

1. The Pope criticizes those who make "false promises," trying to establish a "kingdom of good" in this world that is "guaranteed to last forever." What is the difference between pursuing these false hopes and working to make the world a better place?

2. Take numbers 26 and 27 to prayer with you, and make their words the fuel for an extended period of reflection and meditation.

3. How does your own experience confirm Benedict's words about love in these two sections?

Prayer Prompts

1. Ask God, whom the Pope calls "Life itself and Love itself," to help you to know more truly his love for you and for the world.

2. Reflect prayerfully on the passages about love and life that the Pope cites in this chapter: Romans 8:38–39; Galatians 2:20; John 10:10, 13:1, 17:3, and 19:30.

3. Any Christian would do well to reflect on the lengthy quotation by St. Augustine at the beginning of number 29,

giving thought to how each of these duties can be carried out in daily life. Priests and bishops in particular might draw rich nourishment and a healthy challenge from Augustine's words.

Putting It into Practice

How is God calling you to express your awareness of his love by becoming ever more truly a person *for others?* In what ways might you more concretely serve your spouse, your family, your community, or the Church?

Settings for Learning and Practicing Hope

The Pope divides section eight into three meaty parts: on prayer; action and suffering; and judgment. Because Benedict offers us here so much worthwhile material for reflection, we'll look at each of its three parts separately.

I. PRAYER AS A SCHOOL OF HOPE

"When no one listens to me anymore, God still listens to me. When I can no longer talk to anyone or call upon anyone, I can always talk to God." These simple words could have been written by a frustrated teenager, a cloistered nun, or a lonely senior citizen. Some struggles transcend all boundaries of generation and gender; they are simply part of being human.

The Pope makes these words his own as he opens section eight, the encyclical's longest, highlighting "some of the 'settings' in which we can learn in practice about hope and its exercise."

A Man of Hope

In the first part, on prayer, we're introduced to Cardinal Francis Xavier Nguyen Van Thuan. His story is one you'll want to know. Nguyen Van Thuan was born in Vietnam in 1928, into a family that had already suffered greatly for its faith. He became a priest in 1953. After studies in Rome and work as a teacher and rector of the seminary in Nha Trang, he was named the archbishop of Saigon in April 1975. Within a week, the city fell to the Viet Cong. His faith, his position, and his family connections to the assassinated South Vietnamese leader Ngo Dinh Diem made him an obvious target for the Communist government. He was arrested and imprisoned without a trial. His jail sentence would last thirteen years, nine of them in solitary confinement.

During these prison years, Cardinal Nguyen Van Thuan scribbled prayers and reflections on scraps of paper that he persuaded his guards to give him. So these papers would not be taken from him, especially when he was finally released, he wrote in Italian and put a cover on them marked "Foreign Language Study." This collection of prison prayers was published as a book in 2002 with the title *Prayers of Hope, Words of Courage*.[9] It's the book Pope Benedict refers to in number 32. It contains ninety prayers, most no more than a page long, written in simple sentences that could serve as rich spiritual nourishment for almost anyone. They are evidence of the close relationship Nguyen Van Thuan maintained with Jesus and Mary throughout his prison years. Love, service, and holiness are other common themes throughout the book.

Nguyen Van Thuan was finally released from prison in 1988 and immediately ordered out of his country. At the Vatican, Pope John Paul II welcomed him and put him in charge of the Pontifical Council for Justice and Peace. The Pope asked him to preach his Lenten retreat in 2000. These reflections were later published in book form as *Testimony of Hope*.[10] Benedict refers to this book in number 34 as "his book of spiritual exercises."

John Paul II named Nguyen Van Thuan a cardinal in 2001, before the Vietnamese prelate died of cancer in Rome in 2002. The official cause for his beatification and canonization was opened five years later, as quickly as canon law would allow.[11]

Prayer as Hope

To identify "the intimate relationship between prayer and hope," Benedict turns again to St. Augustine, who spoke of prayer as "an exercise of desire." It expresses our longing for God, and Benedict offers a down-to-earth illustration from St. Augustine to explain why that longing so often seems unfulfilled when we pray. (It's good to know that a spiritual giant like St. Augustine experienced this frustration, too!)

What follows in number 33 is a succinct primer on prayer—what our prayer needs to be and what we must avoid allowing it to become. Finally, the Pope encourages us to make the great prayers of the Church, the saints, and the Church's liturgy part of our personal prayer as well. In this way, we open ourselves to wider horizons and richer nourishment than our own personal experience and spirituality.

Reflection Questions

1. Cardinal Nguyen Van Thuan wrote from prison, "For the love of Christ, a Christian accepts hatred if it comes, and resists sin, laziness, mediocrity, and injustice."[12] Fortunately, most of us do not live in a society in which our faith literally endangers our lives. But have you ever experienced any "hatred" as a result of your faith? In what way? How do you respond to it?

2. Have you ever experienced prayer as an "exercise of desire"? If so, how have you found that desire fulfilled in prayer? And how have you not?

Prayer Prompts

1. Remember that hope, as a theological virtue, is a divine gift, something we receive rather than achieve. But our receptivity to God's gifts can affect "how much" of it we're able to receive. In other words, if we lack hope, maybe it's not because God hasn't given us much, but that we haven't opened ourselves to what God is offering. In your prayer, ask the Spirit to help you open yourself generously and completely to the gift of hope.

2. Make your prayer an expression of your longing for God. Pray Psalm 42.

3. Pray with Cardinal Nguyen Van Thuan:

> Prayer is the breath of the soul.
> Without prayer, the soul suffocates.
> Through prayer, I live in you, Lord.
> I live in you as a baby in its mother's womb
> with its breath united to hers
> and its heart beating in rhythm with hers.[13]

Putting It into Practice

Do you have a regular time of prayer each day? If not, consider keeping a daily appointment with Jesus, one that you zealously defend against encroachments from other activities and obligations.

II. ACTION AND SUFFERING AS SETTINGS FOR LEARNING HOPE

What are your hopes? We've all got them.

Some of mine are big ones. I want to raise happy and good kids, to keep my marriage strong and healthy, to be a great high school teacher. I'd love to think that my writing projects, like the one you're reading now, help to spread the Gospel in the world just a little. I have other hopes, ones that are much smaller in the scheme of things. I want to have some of my paychecks left over to enjoy after all the bills are paid, to find a good book to read, to lose twenty pounds.

The Great Hope

Working toward fulfilling our hopes, says the Pope, "is hope in action." But there's hope and then there's hope. And the theological virtue of hope, Christian hope, directs us way beyond all of our "small" hopes. It turns our gaze to "the great hope that cannot be destroyed." Here, in the Pope's words, is hope in a nutshell:

> It is important to know that I can always continue to hope, even if in my own life, or the historical period in which I am living, there seems to be nothing left to hope for. Only the great certitude of hope that my own life and history in general, despite all failures, are held firm by the indestructible power of Love, and that this gives them their meaning and importance, only this kind of hope can then give the courage to act and persevere. (no. 35)

Benedict makes an interesting point about the way Christians today often speak of "building God's kingdom on earth," usually meaning our efforts for a peaceful and just society. It's God's kingdom, though, not ours. If we think we can build that, we're only fooling ourselves, and we just end up with our *own* kingdom, which will always falter and fail. God's kingdom is a gift, "the response to our hope." We should see our efforts to make the world better as making ourselves and the world *more open* to the kingdom that God wants to build among us. The difference is crucial, not just semantic.

A Hymn of Praise in the Pain

The Pope turns to suffering. He begins by insisting that helping to reduce suffering in the world is "among the fundamental requirements of the Christian life and every truly human life." In our suffering and the suffering we see around us, we come face to face with how very vulnerable we are, how limited in power. God's entering into the history of humanity and into humanity's suffering, however, brings "hope for the world's healing," which is, however, still not completely fulfilled.

Benedict's words here are uncomplicated and need little explanation. They cut like a surgeon's scalpel to the heart of a modern problem. "It is when we attempt to avoid suffering by withdrawing from anything that might involve hurt, when we try to spare ourselves the effort and pain of pursuing truth, love, and goodness, that we drift into a life of emptiness, in which there may be almost no pain, but the dark sensation of meaninglessness and abandonment is all the greater" (no. 37).

This is not the first time the Pope has put his finger on this problem. In his 1977 book *Eschatology: Death and Eternal Life*, Joseph Ratzinger wrote, "The person who does not confront life refuses his life. Flight from suffering is flight from life."[14]

The Pope pauses to consider the witness of Paul Le-Bao-Tinh, a native of Vietnam who was martyred for his faith in 1857. Like Cardinal Nguyen Van Thuan more than a century after him, Le-Bao-Tinh spent time in a Vietnamese prison, and the witness of his hope and courage has been preserved for us in the words he wrote from within its walls. Pope John Paul II canonized him, along with a group of 117 martyrs of Vietnam, in 1988 (the same year, in fact, that Cardinal Nguyen Van Thuan was released from thirteen years of imprisonment and exiled from his country).

The lengthy quotation from a prison letter of Le-Bao-Tinh offers a luminous witness to suffering: when it is experienced by one who is rich in hope, and even when suffering is unjustly inflicted, it can become "despite everything, a hymn of praise."

The Pope then calls us a step farther outside ourselves. Having found meaning in our own suffering, we are called to suffer with others, both to offer comfort and to help them find meaning in their own suffering. Two words that perhaps we use a little too loosely in discussing suffering point the way here: consolation and compassion.

The first three letters in both words, *con-* and *com-*, come from the Latin word for "with." The Latin *solatio* is aloneness or solitude. Consolation, then, goes far beyond merely offering a few kind words to someone who suffers. It means being *with* another person in the solitude that always seems to be part of suffering. Compassion, too, has a depth of meaning. The Latin word *passio* means suffering (and so we speak of the Passion that Christ endured before his death). To offer compassion to those who are hurting means to *suffer with* them, to accompany them through their dark moments.

So real hope leads to real action. It compels us to join in the suffering we see around us, to help relieve it, yes, but also simply to accompany those who suffer, to be present with them in their pain. It is not that those whose eyes are most focused on God are least focused on the world and its pain. On the contrary, some of the greatest mystics and lovers of God spent themselves in the task of relieving and joining themselves to the world's suffering. Christian history offers more examples than I have room to list here, but among them would surely be Rose of Lima, Peter Claver, Vincent de Paul, John Baptist de la Salle, Marie Marguerite d'Youville, and Pier Giorgio

Frassati. Closer to our own time, Padre Pio and Mother Teresa of Calcutta are perfect examples as well.

Offer It Up

Closing this section, Benedict the professor steps aside and Benedict the pastor comes forward, offering some simple spiritual wisdom for daily living. He reminds us of a practice that used to be a common part of Catholic life but has fallen into disuse. Not so long ago, almost all Catholics old enough to learn their multiplication tables also learned the practice of "offering up" one's sufferings to God, uniting them to the suffering of Jesus on the cross and so drawing down powerful grace upon the world. This practice helped even children or uneducated people transform their suffering from simply a bad experience to be endured into something with real meaning and purpose. Somewhere along the way, we forgot about this practice, and we're all spiritually poorer because of it.

One pastor who never forgot the practice was Cardinal John O'Connor, who served as the archbishop of New York from 1984 until his death in 2000. Cardinal O'Connor never missed a chance to remind people of the power of offering one's sufferings. Because he did it so well, he's worth quoting at length. Here's a passage from a column he wrote for New York's archdiocesan newspaper:

> My belief in the tremendous potential of suffering ... began in early childhood, with the standard reply given by my mother and father to my complaints about a toothache, an earache, or a rainstorm that ruined a long-anticipated day at the beach, a very rare day, indeed, in our fam-

ily. "Offer it up!" God will use your pain and your disappointment for His own purposes....

The power of suffering is incalculable. I consider the sick and dying of the Archdiocese of New York, those eaten by cancer, shattered by AIDS, convulsed by seizures, isolated by mental disorders, distorted by uncontrollable spasms —I consider them ... indescribably valuable resources of grace for the Church in New York and for all society.

I repeat what I have said so often: The salvation of the world was not made possible by Christ's teaching or preaching, by His miracles, by His vigor in going up and down the land, often without food, without sleep. The salvation of the world was made possible only by Christ's suffering and death on the Cross. Only when he appeared utterly helpless to the world, totally useless, quivering with agony—only then did He begin to exercise His power, only then did He enter into the fulfillment of His mission on earth. I don't understand it for a fraction of a moment, but it is categorically true.

Neither do I understand how it is that if I unite my sufferings with those of Christ on the Cross—my toothache, or headache, or heartache, my temptations, the guilt I feel over my sins, whatever my sorrow or whatever its cause—I help Christ continue the salvation of the world. I believe this with all my being.[15]

Reflection Questions

1. So what *are* your hopes, big and small?

2. Have you ever heard this idea of offering up suffering? If so, where? Have you ever done it?

3. We try in all kinds of ways today to "withdraw from anything that might involve hurt." How do you see this in your own life or in our society?

Prayer Prompts

1. My book *Saints for Our Times: New Novenas and Prayers* includes a chapter on the 117 Vietnamese martyrs canonized in 1988. Consider praying the original novena in that book, perhaps in preparation for the celebration of their feast day, November 24.

2. The Pope writes, "The true measure of humanity is essentially determined in relationship to suffering and to the suffered." Where do I stand when I evaluate myself by this measure? The questions Benedict poses offer an opportunity for a helpful (though perhaps difficult) examination of conscience: "Is the other [person] important enough to warrant my becoming, on his account, a person who suffers? Does truth matter to me enough to make suffering worthwhile? Is the promise of love so great that it justifies the gift of myself?"

3. What am I suffering in my own life that I can offer up?

Putting It into Practice

This section is a strong call to enter into the suffering of those around us. We don't have to travel to faraway lands to find it. Look around you, at your family, your friends, your co-workers, your city or town. Pick one place you see suffering that you can personally address. It needn't be a lifetime commitment. Just think about something for today, for this week. And remember, the Pope is asking us not only to help relieve the suffering, but also to enter into it. It's easy and good to send a check to a food pantry. But to allow the Pope's message to truly sink in, ask yourself, "How can I *accompany* the sufferer

I have in mind in his suffering? How can I be with her in the midst of it?"

———— ❧ ————

III. JUDGMENT AS A SETTING FOR LEARNING AND PRACTICING HOPE

In a final, fascinating part of section eight, Pope Benedict turns our attention to the final judgment, which Christ promised would accompany his Second Coming. Into his discussion of this doctrine the Pope weaves reflections on architecture, art, and twentieth-century Jewish philosophy as well. He also offers a few thoughts on apologetics. His point in all of this is to present the Last Judgment that Christians await as "the decisive image of hope."

Depicting Damnation

Benedict's reflections on early Christian Church architecture and later artistic depictions of the Last Judgment are easy enough to follow. To see what he means by the "ominous and frightening aspects" of the Last Judgment holding "more fascination for artists than the splendor of hope," you need only check out a few examples. Medieval and early modern artists always depict both the heavenly reward of those who are saved and the damnation of those who aren't, but somehow the damnation side is always more interesting. Consider:

○ Luca Signorelli's famous last judgment frescoes in the cathedral church (or *duomo*) of Orvieto, Italy, painted around 1500, depict both *The Elect* and *The Damned*. While the damned are undergoing the assaults of hideous green, winged demons, the elect look like they're standing around waiting for a bus (albeit naked).

○ In Hans Memling's fifteenth-century *Last Judgment Triptych*, the damned are tumbling and burning in a dark inferno as nasty black demons torment them with sticks. The saved, meanwhile, are filing off to church (the joy being that they get to do it naked?), greeted by an unsmiling (and fully dressed) St. Peter.

○ Jan Van Eyck's fifteenth-century *Last Judgment* in oil shows the damned suspended upside down from the crotch of a huge skeleton and being attacked by ugly monsters, while the saved seem to be joining (naked again) in a town meeting with the saints.

Those are just a few. (For links to images of each of these works, see my Web site, www.barrymichaelsbooks.com.) In almost all medieval and early modern depictions of the Last Judgment (including Michelangelo's famous Sistine Chapel version), the greatest delight of the saved seems to be that they avoided being put on the other side of the painting.

Atheism for Moral Reasons

As for modern times, the Pope says that the longing for ultimate justice, or perhaps frustration that it seems not to exist, has led to a particular version of atheism over the past 200 years. He identifies its line of thought without flinching: "A world marked by so much injustice, innocent suffering, and cynicism of power cannot be the work of a good God. A God with responsibility for such a world would not be a just God, much less a good God. It is for the sake of morality that this God has to be contested" (no. 42).

The problem with this is that humanity *can't* provide ultimate justice, and our attempts to impose it have often been disastrous. Stalinist Marxism provides a clear example here. "A world which has to create its own justice is a world without hope," the Pope says.

Here the Pope mentions Theodor Adorno and Max Horkheimer. They were the leading figures from the Frankfurt School, a group of German philosophers, mostly Jewish, who worked from the time of the Second World War and through the following decades. Looking squarely at the brutalities endured by the innocent in the world, Adorno and Horkheimer realized that speaking of real justice was nonsense if it did not include undoing all the heinous injustices of the past as well as the present. In other words, only bringing the dead back to life to "give them their due" could ever really "make things right." Of course, Adorno and Horkheimer have arrived, via a non-Christian route, at precisely what Christianity proposes in its expectation of the resurrection of the body and the Last Judgment.

The insight explains why, as Benedict says, "faith in the Last Judgment is first and foremost hope." It is the only way that the scales can ever really be balanced, that things can truly be set right, and that the injustices that humans experience or inflict upon one another can definitively be undone.

The Fire that Burns and Saves

Here Benedict offers some advice to those who are engaged in Christian apologetics, which presents the reasonableness of faith to those who question or reject it. He suggests that our innate desire for justice, which is rarely fulfilled during our earthly lives, "constitutes the essential argument, or in any case the strongest argument, in favor of faith in eternal life" (no. 43). It is "an important motive for believing that man was made for eternity."

Benedict offers some of his most compelling words in his discussion of purgatory. Here, too, apologists will find helpful insights. Citing passages of Scripture, the work of the Russian writer Fyodor Dostoevsky, the Greek philosopher Plato, and everyday human experience, he demonstrates why the existence of purgatory makes sense.

Benedict has made this basic argument before, in his 1977 book, *Eschatology: Death and Eternal Life*. While some people may truly reject God definitely, and others may live lives of extraordinary holiness, most of us fall somewhere in the ambiguous middle, muddling through life with good intentions but weaknesses that often get the better of us. The thrust of our lives may be for God and goodness, but, as Joseph Ratzinger wrote in *Eschatology*, "[i]t may be that the basic decision of a human being is covered over by layers of secondary decisions and needs to be dug free."[16]

Without purgatory (the word means purification), these sins simply would no longer matter when we die. But the doctrine of purgatory says that our souls are purified of these sins in "the fire which both burns and saves." The Pope suggests it might be better to think of purgatory as our encounter with Christ himself at the end of our lives (rather than a place), an encounter that "transforms and frees us, allowing us to become truly ourselves."

The truths of God's mercy and God's justice, then, are not a contradiction, but a paradox. The tension is resolved. It is a doctrine that brims with hope: "the way we live our lives is not immaterial, but our defilement does not stain us forever if we have at least continued to reach out towards Christ, towards truth, and towards love" (no. 47).

Benedict closes this compelling section with further reflections on the possibility of helping by our prayers those who have died. Here, too, apologists and teachers should take note.

Reflection Questions

1. It's so easy to criticize long-dead artists! Use some creativity and imagination now. How *could* an artist depict the splendor of heaven with the same degree of compelling, stunning imagery as the pains of hell were once so commonly put on canvases, altarpieces, and church walls?

2. Have you ever been tempted to atheism for the reasons Pope Benedict describes here? Do you know anybody who is an atheist for this reason?

Prayer Prompts

1. Read and ponder number 1040 in the *Catechism of the Catholic Church*.

2. The hit song "I Can Only Imagine" by Mercy Me would be a great resource to include in your prayer time as you reflect on this section of *Spe Salvi*. If you're more classically inclined, an image of Michelangelo's *Last Judgment* would also offer some fuel for prayer. Or, if you're an artist yourself, come up with your own song, poem, or drawing to express the Pope's ideas here. Make your own art a prayer.

3. Pray for your loved ones who have died.

Putting It into Practice

Though having Masses offered for the dead used to be a common part of Catholic life, some Catholics today have no familiarity at all with this practice. It remains a significant way to pray for those who have gone before us. (Because God and those who have died live outside the stream of human time, in an eternal "now," it's even reasonable to think that our prayers can be of help to people who died long ago.) Stop by your parish rectory and arrange for a Mass to be offered for a loved one who has died. Be aware before you go that a financial offering (which is called a stipend and is typically ten dollars), is usually an expected part of scheduling a Mass; it's your way of joining yourself to the prayer, even if you are not able to participate in the Mass when it is celebrated.

———— ❧ ————

Mary, Star of Hope

Already in *Spe Salvi*, the Pope has spoken several times of "the star of hope rising." It's been a general reference to the Christian hope we bear, which is present and active in our lives and in the world. (See nos. 37, 39, and 48.)

Now, however, the Pope presents "the star of hope" as a person. The phrase becomes a title he addresses to Mary. The two points he makes here explain why.

Lighting Our Way

Mary is the personification of the Old Testament, the writings of the Israelite people that shimmer with hope because the entire history they represent was one of hope. As a faithful member of that people, Mary lived a life that was, Benedict writes, "thoroughly imbued" with those writings, and because she was the mother of Jesus, it was through her that "the hope of the ages became reality."

She is also the Star of Hope because she is a light to mark our way along the sometimes difficult journeys of our lives, journeys during which we might very well be tempted to allow our hope to falter. This woman whose living hope became a courageous "yes" to God that "opened the door of our world to God himself," shows us the possibility and the power of hope.

After a brief opening paragraph, the majority of this section of *Spe Salvi* is a prayer. It is a long, rich, and beautiful prayer through which the Pope weaves many themes and events related to Christian hope. To give it only a cursory reading as we finish the letter would be a mistake.

One way to begin to draw out its richness might be simply to take a look at the many titles and descriptions of Jesus and of Mary that the Pope uses in his letter.

JESUS

- ○ true light
- ○ hope of Israel
- ○ hope of the ages
- ○ hope of the world
- ○ servant of God
- ○ sign of contradiction
- ○ Savior of the world
- ○ heir of David
- ○ Son of God

MARY

- ○ Mother of God
- ○ Star of the Sea

○ Star of hope
○ Ark of the Covenant
○ handmaid of the Lord
○ image of the Church
○ mother of believers
○ Mother of hope
○ Holy Mary

The Pope speaks of us, too, the followers of Christ. He uses one description of us in particular, repeated several times. We are "the family of Jesus," the family of the One who is the hope of the world. Can members of a family like that ever really lack a sense of the goodness, the meaning, and the direction of life?

Reflection Questions

1. The Pope touches on many moments and images of Mary's hope here. Is there one with which you can especially identify?

2. Who else has served for you as one of the "lights close by—people who shine with [Christ's] light and so guide us along our way" (no. 49)?

Prayer Prompts

1. This entire section is a call to prayer. Certainly it would be worthwhile to spend a good chunk of prayer time simply reading and reflecting on number 50 slowly and quietly. You might also break it up into a week of prayer time, taking five or six sentences a day. Finally, consider using only those two

lists above, the titles and descriptions of Jesus and Mary that the Pope uses, as springboards for prayer and reflection.

Putting It into Practice

Hope, we have seen, makes us people for others. Real hope is hope that we share. Is there someone with whom you could discuss what you've gained from reading *Spe Salvi* (maybe without ever mentioning the letter itself)? Is there someone to whom you might pass along your copy of the encyclical or forward an Internet link to the letter? (You can find the encyclical letter at www.vatican.va/holy_father/benedict_xvi and click on "encyclicals.")

Notes

1. www.vatican.va/holy_father; click on "John Paul II," "speehes," "1992," and "May," and scroll down to "To Pilgrims in Rome for the Beatification of Sr. Giuseppina Bakhita."

2. www.vatican.va/holy_father; click on "John Paul II," "homilies," and "1993," and scroll down to "10 Februaray 1993, Eucharistic Celebration in Honor of Blessed Josephine Bakhita, Khartoum."

3. Available from Pauline Books & Media: www.pauline.org or 1-800-876-4463.

4. Numbers following excerpts from *Spe Salvi* refer to the paragraph in the document cited, not the page number.

5. Here I'm using the *New American Bible* translation. *The New Revised Standard Version*, which I've used for other scriptural quotes in this guide, offers a translation that reflects the tendency Pope Benedict is criticizing here. The *NAB*, on the other hand, suggests an understanding of the Greek closer to the one Benedict proposes.

6. The same conclusions about the meaning of the Greek words can be found, for example, in *The Collegeville Bible Commentary* (Collegeville, MN: Liturgical Press, 1989), 1259; and *The New Jerome Biblical Commentary* (Englewood Cliffs, NJ: Prentice Hall, 1990), 939-949.

7. For more on Ratzinger's thoughts on de Lubac, see Henri de Lubac, *Catholicism: Christ and the Common Destiny of Man* (San Francisco: Ignatius, 1988), 11.

8. Especially helpful here was William Bush, *To Quell the Terror: The Mystery of the Vocation of the Sixteen Carmelites of Compiegne Guillotined July 17, 1794* (Washington, DC: ICS Books, 1999).

9. Francis Xavier Nguyen Van Thuan, *Prayers of Hope, Words of Courage* (Boston: Pauline Books & Media, 2002), ix-x.

10. Francis Xavier Nguyen Van Thuan, *Tesstimony of Hope: The Spiritual Exercises of Pope John Paul II* (Boston: Pauline Books & Media, 2000).

11. To explore Cardinal Nguyen Van Thuan's remarkable story more deeply, see Andre Nguyen Van Chau's biography, *The Miracle of Hope: Political Prisoner, Prophet of Hope* (Boston: Pauline Books & Media, 2003).

12. Nguyen Van Thuan, *Prayers of Hope, Words of Courage*, 19.

13. Ibid., 114.

14. Joseph Ratzinger, *Eschatology: Death and Eternal Life* (Washington, D.C.: Catholic University of America Press, 1988), 103. On this topic, pages 101–103 are especially worth a look.

15. John Joseph O'Connor, *On Being Catholic* (New York: Alba House, 1994), 63-64.

16. Ratzinger, *Eschatology: Death and Eternal Life*, 219.

Pauline
BOOKS & MEDIA

The Daughters of St. Paul operate book and media centers at the following addresses. Visit, call or write the one nearest you today, or find us on the World Wide Web, www.pauline.org

CALIFORNIA

3908 Sepulveda Blvd, Culver City, CA
90230 310-397-8676

2650 Broadway Street, Redwood City,
CA 94063 650-369-4230

5945 Balboa Avenue, San Diego, CA
92111 858-565-9181

FLORIDA

145 S.W. 107th Avenue, Miami, FL
33174 305-559-6715

HAWAII

1143 Bishop Street, Honolulu,
HI 96813 808-521-2731

Neighbor Islands call: 866-521-2731

ILLINOIS

172 North Michigan Avenue,
Chicago, IL 60601 312-346-4228

LOUISIANA

4403 Veterans Memorial Blvd,
Metairie, LA 70006 504-887-7631

MASSACHUSETTS

885 Providence Hwy, Dedham, MA
02026 781-326-5385

MISSOURI

9804 Watson Road, St. Louis, MO
63126 314-965-3512

NEW JERSEY

561 U.S. Route 1, Wick Plaza, Edison,
NJ 08817 732-572-1200

NEW YORK

150 East 52nd Street, New York, NY
10022 212-754-1110

PENNSYLVANIA

9171-A Roosevelt Blvd, Philadelphia,
PA 19114 215-676-9494

SOUTH CAROLINA

243 King Street, Charleston,
SC 29401 843-577-0175

TENNESSEE

4811 Poplar Avenue, Memphis, TN
38117 901-761-2987

TEXAS

114 Main Plaza, San Antonio,
TX 78205 210-224-8101

VIRGINIA

1025 King Street, Alexandria,
VA 22314 703-549-3806

CANADA

3022 Dufferin Street, Toronto,
ON M6B 3T5 416-781-9131

¡También somos su fuente para libros, videos y música en español!